Dogs

by Helen Frost

Consulting Editor: Gail Saunders-Smith, Ph.D.

Consultant: Jennifer Zablotny, D.V.M.,
Member, American Animal Hospital Association

Pebble Books

an imprint of Capstone Press
Mankato, Minnesota

Pebble Books are published by Capstone Press
151 Good Counsel Drive, P.O. Box 669, Mankato, Minnesota 56002
www.capstonepress.com

Printed in the United States of America.
3 4 5 6 7 8 11 10 09 08 07 06

Library of Congress Cataloging-in-Publication Data
Frost, Helen, 1949–
    Dogs/by Helen Frost.
    p. cm.—(All about pets)
    Includes bibliographical references and index.
    Summary: Simple text and photographs present the features and care of dogs.
    ISBN 0-7368-0656-3 (hardcover)
    ISBN 0-7368-8784-9 (softcover)
    1. Dogs—Juvenile literature. [1. Dogs. 2. Pets.] I. Title. II. All about pets
(Mankato, Minn.)
SF426.5 .F76 2001
636.7—dc21
                                                        00-022987

Note to Parents and Teachers

The All About Pets series supports national science standards for
units on the diversity and unity of life. This book describes domesti-
cated dogs and illustrates what they need from their owners. The
photographs support emergent readers in understanding the text.
The repetition of words and phrases helps emergent readers learn
new words. This book also introduces emergent readers to subject-
specific vocabulary words, which are defined in the Words to Know
section. Emergent readers may need assistance to read some words
and to use the Table of Contents, Words to Know, Read More,
Internet Sites, and Index/Word List sections of the book.

Table of Contents

Pet Dogs..........................5
How Dogs Look 7
What Dogs Need 15

Words to Know.................22
Read More......................23
Internet Sites 23
Index/Word List...............24

4

Dogs are pets.

Dogs have four paws.

Dogs have long hair or short hair.

Most dogs have tails.

12

Dogs have pointed teeth.

Dogs need food
and water.

Dogs need to be brushed.

Dogs need a bed.

Dogs need a place
to run and play.

Words to Know

bed—a place to sleep; a dog needs its own bed; dog beds can be special blankets, pads, or pillows.

brush—to smooth hair using an object with bristles and a handle; pet owners should brush dogs' hair a few times each week.

food—something that people, animals, and plants need to stay alive and grow; pet owners should feed only dog food to dogs.

paw—the foot of an animal; most animals with paws have four feet and claws; pet owners should clip dogs' claws when they get too long.

pet—a tame animal kept for company or pleasure

tail—the part at the back end of an animal's body; dogs may have long or short tails.

teeth—the white bony parts of a mouth; dogs use their teeth to bite and chew; they have long, pointed teeth in the front of their mouths.

Read More

Evans, Mark. *The Complete Guide to Puppy Care.* Animal Care. New York: Howell Book House, 1997.

Gutman, Bill. *Becoming Your Dog's Best Friend.* Pet Friends. Brookfield, Conn.: Millbrook Press, 1996.

Schaefer, Lola. *Family Pets.* Families. Mankato, Minn.: Pebble Books, 1999.

Starke, Katherine. *Dogs and Puppies.* First Pets. London: Usborne Publishing, 1998.

Internet Sites

FactHound offers a safe, fun way to find Internet sites related to this book.

Go to *www.facthound.com*

He'll fetch the best sites for you!

Index/Word List

are, 5
bed, 19
brushed, 17
food, 15
four, 7
hair, 9
have, 7, 9, 11, 13
long, 9
most, 11
need, 15, 17, 19, 21

paws, 7
pets, 5
place, 21
play, 21
pointed, 13
run, 21
short, 9
tails, 11
teeth, 13
water, 15

Word Count: 44
Early-Intervention Level: 5

Editorial Credits
Martha E. H. Rustad, editor; Linda Clavel, designer; Jodi Theisen and Katy Kudela, photo researchers; Crystal Graf, photo editor

Photo Credits
Index Stock Imagery, 1, 4
Jean M. Fogle, 8
Jim Cummins/FPG International LLC, cover
Kent and Donna Dannen, 6, 10, 20
Norvia Behling, 16, 18
Photo Network/Scott Loy, 12; Myrleen Cate, 14

The author thanks the children's section staff at the Allen County Public Library in Fort Wayne, Indiana, for research assistance. The author also thanks Nancy T. Whitesell, D.V.M., at St. Joseph Animal Hospital in Fort Wayne, Indiana.